Journey to My Identity

From a Poetic Standpoint

Jazmin Wilson

Jazmin Wilson

Visit my website www.SpeakEasyPoets.com

Printed in the United States of America

First Edition

ISBN 978-0-578-03069-2

This book is dedicated to love and life for taking me by storm, magnifying the true beauty in me, and enabling me to believe in the impossible.

I give great thanks to GOD for allowing me to use the gift that he has blessed me with and to my family as well as extended family (i.e. close friends) for always supporting me and giving me words of encouragement.

"Naked I came from my mother's womb, and naked I shall return there. The Lord gave and the Lord has taken away. Blessed be the name of the Lord." Job 1:21

www.SpeakEasyPoets.com

Contents

Just Listen

To my imagination; when will it all end?
I keep telling myself to speak with my mind through words and not always with
my pen.
Time and time again;
I'm filled with feelings from within.
You ask...what's on my mind?
Just some things that seem unjust and undying
You say you care. Do you really?
Cause all I want you to do is just listen.
Listen to my words, my actions, and my feelings from within.
But most importantly
Listen to the things that I write with my pen.

Ay-eye-dee-ess (Part 1)

The rumor is that black women are highly admired because of our full face and
lips
Hips
Shape
Grace
Strength

So tell me….do you like what you see?
But hold up…this just in….
There's a disappearance of beautiful audacious black women like me
And no more lively attraction for our men

There's been a crisis
I read an article that validated the fact that we were the fastest growing group
with "ay-eye-dee-ess"
So while you undress me with your eyes think about this
I am a 25 year old Black woman
And in the United States, black women between the ages of 25 to 44 are 13 times
more likely to die from this disease than any other race

We don't get the opportunity to chase our dreams
because we're too busy trying to stay clean
from the defiled wretched stench of this tasteless truth

So what do we do?

In order for me to even make it to the age of 44 I must protect myself
and encourage others to protect themselves
And by doing so I will continue to protest the fact
that they can't forget about "ay-eye-dee-ess"
And by doing that…I will live beyond my 50's and 60's
And yes…
hopefully long enough to see my great grandkids grow into their teens

These odds seem a whole lot better than those of that 25, 44, and 13

Backtrack

Sometimes I think about the things of my past
And even though I don't like to look back
There comes a time when I have to unveil the mask
And retrace the steps of my path.

What if I would have done things differently
Or acted a certain way.
What if I would have significantly done things on a different day
What if I didn't have to witness the beatings and mistreatings of my mother's
significant other-lover-friend formally known as the "husband" and currently
known as my father
What if my father was more of a father instead of a disciplinarian
And what if my father wasn't such a lecturer
Would I still know the things that I know and think about the things that most
folks don't
What if my father never educated me about men
Would I still be as cautious as I am when choosing my next male-friend
Even if half of them were alleged scrubs…that just means that I didn't listen

If my father was never really my father then I probably wouldn't be as litigious,
opinionated, or creative as I am.
Cause my father met my mother and they made me who I am.
And honestly…that's one of the greatest things they could have ever done.

What if my little sister was never born
Would she still be considered one of my closest friends
What if my best friends weren't just that….my best-friends
Would I still be able to say that I have the greatest friends who I can call my
sisters
What if my mother wasn't my life coach
Would I have a different take and approach on life
Or would I make bountiful mistakes and add continued stress to my strife
Would I still have grown up to be this determined young women that my mother
molded me to be

What if my step-dad wasn't my stepped up dad
Would I have been as worried as I was when he spent a year in Iraq
Or would I be so glad to see him, know him and call him my dad

Would I remain that little girl who wasn't familiar with him and every time he came around I would always say to my mom "he at the door" as if he had no name.

Sam Cook said "a change was gonna to come"....
It came...and it went...that's why I'm sitting here thinking back on how my life begun.

The Blood of Another Man

One thing that I will never be able to understand
Is how a man could stand to live with the blood of another man on his hands
How is it possible to walk away and live a normal life
After looking into a victims eyes
And watching them turn to a lifeless stone cold dying pale white

The only blood that I can bare to carry on my skin
Is the blood of Jesus because he died for my sins
So with that being said…I proclaim it hard to intake
The fact that one man
Can take,
The life of another man
And never be able the wash that sin from his hands

Darkness

When darkness falls…
I see you
And…
You see me
We lust after each other completely.
Believe me; I understand we carry on this friendly relationship during the day,
But when darkness falls…
You caress me…
And…
I test your dependability.
I don't trust easily.

You keep telling me
But I don't comprehend your spoken word.
Your touch tries to suppress my insecurity
And…
… I jump.

I jump from your touch.
Leaving you with many thoughts of…
"Did I…"
"Could I…"
"Should I…"
"…stop!"
But I don't want you too.
I have grown fond of this new found, tempting, teasing touch.
And…
When dawn cracks,
I go on as if nothing ever happened, nothing even matters.

When darkness falls…

Ay-eye-dee-ess (part 2)

Sweet Africa...
>Some call you the motherland
>But I see you as another land
>Devastated from the statistics of your incubated plague

The motherland that gave birth to another man
>That contributed to the estimate of 25 million infected with HIV/AIDS
>Decreasing your bitter sweet value and enabling you to
>Unwillingly surrender another one of your residents into the healing

clouds of   heaven
3.2 million new infections in 2007
2.4 million deaths
25.8 million victims
And a 47 year life expectancy
Unexpectedly, babies unable to be innocent infants because they were birthed
into the desolate disease of your beautiful continent

Kenya, Tanzania, Ethiopia, Rwanda, and Uganda to name a few
Ghana, Gambia, Liberia, and Nigeria are all victims too

You give birth to a life that's not worth living
And yet its life that you keep giving

Sweet Africa...
Please tell me the story of your enemies
Cause the colors and pictures on the cover of your book
Don't exactly compare to the content on the inside that describe how many lives
they took

Disconnected

When I get around you boy,
My tears of pain, turn into tears of joy.
My love for you is not to be questioned.
There is no doubt in my mind, you and I were destined.
Destined to be, with all eternity.

When things suddenly change,
You leave me with numerous questions.
Nothings quite the same.
And everyone I talk to, have ran out of suggestions.
At night when I am alone,
I find myself dialing those seven numbers that connect me to your phone.
After a few minutes of ringing and thinking of things to discuss.
I find myself listening to the message that replies, "The person you are trying to reach is unavailable to answer the phone. Please leave a message after the tone."

Some of the things that I say might seem a little cruel and superfluous.
But to tell you the truth,
I worry less about me, individually.
And worry more about us.
Trying to depict on whether what you feel for me is love or lust.
Thinking of the negative things dealing with our relationship.
I realize that I'm not being confident.
But I am better than that.
So I think of the positive, and come out as being dominant.

I feel there is a cord between us.
This little cord that keeps us connected.
This is what keeps me loving you; trusting you; lusting after you passionately, emotionally, and indefinitely.
It is you that I adore,
And this is what keeps me loving you more.

The only thing that scares me,
Is that one day you'll mess up, or give up.
And that little cord will be cut up.
Leaving us disconnected.

Everlasting Smile

Luscious to the eye
Beautiful in sight
Inhale, Exhale....I try
Breathtaking, but just right
Honey dipped
Tantalizing lips
Attractive all the while
Caramelized everlasting smile

I Am

I am your reason for living.
A woman of many intellects.
I am your educator.
I'll teach you things and give you an education worth giving.

I am your protector.
Defending you from all harm of any kind.
I am your friend.
Ready to listen to your problems and give you advice at all times.

I am your companion, your significant other.
Giving you nothing but love in return.
I am your family.
Showing you when I care and when I am concerned.

So when times get hard and you try to convince me that you are the man.
I stand and I say;
I am your reason for living,
You educator, you protector, your friend, your companion, and your family.
Soul sister on the inside, black woman on the outside.
Still I stand.
I am the woman who molded you into that man.

Picture Perfect

Paint me a portrait of 1000 words
Pave way for me to visualize your many thoughts
Transpire your feelings into melodic sounds of blissful peace
A symphony of invaluable freedom and civil rights speeches
Rectify this broken mirror of repetitive societal destruction

I believe it was the King who said he had a dream
And the remarkable Hughes who inquired about them being deferred

I refer to it as a movement...far beyond those of the black arts
There are no X's, or Giovanni's who can lawfully analyze what's in your heart...
They have left their distinctive mark by playing a part in the revolution and
allowing their voice to epitomize the evolution of our lives.

Converse your philosophy on racial impurity
And proclaim your dialogue on human security
Give your judgment on the obliteration of AIDS
Present to me a script of logical cures that don't seem unbecoming or jaded
Compose a thorough dissertation on the crisis of Somalia's starvation

Add a few rhymes in your lines...a pinch of intellectual apprehension and use it
Throw in some tunes...some music
Subtract what's disguised and add some facts
A sonnet of reality...and a haiku of personality
Add instruments to your monologue and transform your verses into poems
containing rhythmic dialect.
Construct a poetic collage of freedom, peace, health, wealth...
And label it Picture Perfect.

A Jones for Jazmin

I love rainy days...rainy nights. I'm standing here looking out this big gaping window. Watching this panoply of rain drops hit the pavement. Listening to its distinctive sound as it makes contact with the ground. It's making music while I'm gazing into the night. I feel his presence from behind...his strong arms wrapped around me making me feel as if they're doing a double wrap around my waist because his grip was so tight. Nothing is as pleasant as feeling the warmth of his sweet breathe brush across my neck as his lips move closer... I hear him whisper in my right ear... which sends chills to my left. I feel his heart beat through his chest as it's pressed up against my back...and I don't have to look back...cause I know that he's always going to be there. My feelings and emotions are telling me so...his emotions, and feelings, and affections, and spirit are telling him that he can't let go. And he thinks that I don't know...about how he watches me in my sleep when I'm deep in my beauty slumber...lying there staring at my face in the dark...gliding his finger down my spine and tracing the rose that's tattooed on my back. He thinks I can't feel that? I even noticed the way that he goes out of his way to ask me about my day and how he's always so interested in everything that I have to say. He doesn't think that any women compares to me. He treats me like a queen... he says "good woman are few and far between."

Lost in time

I just wanna disappear…
…and make it as if you never even knew of me.

I don't want you to see me, hear me, or speak of me.
When you wake up in the morning…
I don't even want you to think of me.
When you go to bed at night…
I don't even want you to pray for me.

I don't want to be a memory of your past,
A friend of your present.
Or a possible in your future.

I don't wanna be a maybe…
Or an uncertain.

I used to want to be a definite.
But judging from your hesitation, I can see that I am…
…an indefinite.

I wanna walk away on my journey to a fresh start and a new beginning.
I don't know where I'm going but when I will get there…
I know that I will be innovative,
And rejuvenated.

It's now my time to disappear…
I don't want you to wish for me.
And I don't want you to miss me.

And when the time comes for me to reappear,
And take a step out of **your** fantasy…
into **my** reality.
You will undeniably…
Get to see…
The real me.

That will be the moment where you will stop,
Think,

And realize…
That what you felt was a waste of love, interest, and unison of the minds…
Was lost in your self-interested capsule of time.

Your Everything

I wanna be your everything,
          Love you and never stop loving you,
          Be a part of the reason why you wake up in the morning
          And put one foot in front of the other

I wanna be your definition of true love and ecstasy
          Do things that you never thought you would do
          Say things that you never thought you would say
          And feel things that you never thought you would feel

I wanna be your future
          Some how and in some kinda way, I wanna be your first
          Because being your first in something is considered priceless history
          …And…I wanna make history

I wanna be your best friend
          Tell me your dreams, fears, and secrets
          Tell me what pleases you and what satisfies you
          Tell me… tell me anything because all that I wanna do is listen to you

I wanna be your inspiration
          The subject matter of that really intense love poem
          That voice that you hear when you feel like things are going wrong
          …That's me telling you that I'm here

I wanna be the one
          The one who makes your heart skip a beat
          The one who you get down on your knees for
          The one who matters

I wanna be your everything because my everything is you
My everything is loving you
My everything is love
My everything is your everything

Enchanting…

He speaks soft magical words to me every night
And when morning comes I become high off of him
He is my vision…
…my finished sentence
I breathe his defining spirit
And even if I tried to cleanse myself of his powerful existence
I become empowered by his quintessence of manhood
And my taste buds become fully satisfied from the sweet succulent taste of
happiness

He is that love song that gets stuck in my head
And I'm singing him all throughout the day
Even into the wee hours of the night, in which we call morning
I dance circles around him in my fantasy because my fantasy became actuality
And I can't help but to move to the beat of his love song
He is my enchanted love

Decisions

Decisions…Love you or Leave you

I've given myself to you physically, mentally, & emotionally.
I'm drained of all except one.
Mentally, I must maintain, got to stay on top of my game.

I put forth my all, in order to please you,
But pleasing you seems unfeasible.
As much as I do for you,
When will I get it all back in return?

Why must I do this and that for you?
And you sit back and do a little bit of that for me.

Sometimes I feel as if I'm wasting my time,
But you assure me that my time is well spent.
Why do I continue to fall for the difficult ones?

Loving you is a 24/7 job,
But leaving you takes less than 24 seconds.
Decisions!?!

Love

I want love…
…make my knees shake love…
Quivers, kisses down my back love
Can't get enough of that love
Say my name…whispers in my ear love
Can't stop thinking about you love
Yes, that…when you're sick and tired of messing with those dimes love…
You come running to a diamond…
…in the rough can't get enough love.
Passionate love…
Caring love…
Simple, definitive love

My 25th **(In tribute to my 25th year of living a blessed life)**

This is the year that I make things official
Cause on my 18th is when I declared my initial.
I plan to strike hard and come back with a vengeance.
So on my 25th I'm declaring my follow-up independence.

I declare to always be proud of who I am.
Never telling myself I can't…instead I will and I can.
I declare that the next time I'm criticized by another woman or man.
I will laugh in their faces and say "baby you can't do it like I can."
You ain't got it like how I got it.
You talk it, but I'm about it.
I live, speak, and breathe
What you read in those asinine magazines about being free.
In touch with who you are when it's me you want to be.

I will plummet through your army of chastising comments
Keeping them as war trophies, motivating me to move past this sea of negativity.

Victory will be my goal
Cause failure will be pleasing to all those who vote against me.

This is my proclamation!
I vow never ever to allow myself to be submerged under, drowning from such
insidious acts of quondam friends
and so called friends
and so called men…
and women.
I will teach my future mini me's…
My babies… and their babies.
Cause when I look into their eyes I will see me in them.
And I know it will hurt them more, to know that I couldn't stand up for what I
believed in…
…and I might not get the chance to do this again.
Cause tomorrow is never promised and today is just the beginning.

Wishing I could turn back the hands of time.

These thoughts in my head seem to be driving me crazy…
…daily,

I'm missing you,
Wishing you were here.
Wishing I could turn back the hands of time.
Hoping and praying that I will overcome this pain.

Unfortunately, things will never be the same.
All of these thoughts of you will continue to loiter in my brain.

I wanted you…
…needed you.
Would do anything for you?

No one will have my back like you did,
Encouraged,
Loved,
Or like how I thought you did.

I made a lot of mistakes.
And one of them was taking our relationship for granted.
Not accepting you for who you were and trying to change you.
I thought we were identical, compatible…interchangeable.
thought we understood each other.

Any thoughts of us being apart were elusive.
I figured what we had, was exclusive.

I was too strong of a woman to accept some things
And I had to reap the consequences of a man who just wasn't ready to commit.
One minute I'm making you feel like a king
And the next minute I'm stressing you
Cause you weren't blessing me,
By fulfilling my wants and needs.

If I could have done things differently, we probably would have just been friends
I would still have you in my life and you would still be my best friend.

Narcissism

I'm sensual, seductive, sassy
Classy!
The way that I walk.
The way that I talk.
Or maybe it's these 3 inch stilettos that I rock.

Maybe it's my 27 inch waist that accentuates my shape.
Or…it could be the dark brown tint of my hair
That matches the dark coal black color of my eyes,
That resembles the shape of a medium sized almond that gets me by.

Maybe it's this pecan tan complexion that my mama keeps talkin' about.
The color that's 5 shades lighter than her paper sack brown
And 3 shades darker than my grandmother's yellow bone tone.

Maybe it's the fact that I fit in
Ready and willing to begin,
A group or clique of my own from within,
That fits the standpoint of my preferred friends

I got my cell phone to talk to you whenever I feel like talkin' to you,
Got my iPod so that I don't have to listen to the same music that you do
What I want, what I like, the way I look

The truth of the matter is…
That this is said to be, how my generation really is.
Self loved, self-centered, egotistical, all of the above
Mean the same thing, are one in the same,
Characterized by a generation who could care less about how you perceive them…
Because their too caught up in how others perceive them

Now that's a shame…

Poetry

Poetry is my get-away,
My escape,
My trials and my tribulations.

Poetry is my story,
My struggle,
My strife,
Poetry is my life.

Poetry is my experience,
My love,
My passion,
And my appearance.

Poetry is my emotions,
My feelings,
My mind,
My heart,
My thoughts.
Poetry is my spirit!

…do you hear it?
Poetry is my lyric!

Listen…
Read it…
You can tell that I'm dealing with and speaking about some real shhh…
Feel it…
Sing it…
Dream it…

Poetry is me!
I'm a living, walking, talking poet,
And poetry is all that I know how to be!

Resentment

Why do we, as women, seem to make the mistake of loving someone more than we love ourselves?

I mean, it happens...and I too am guilty of this mistake.

I was always told that in order for someone else to love us...we have to love ourselves first...even if that means putting our "love interest" on the back burner. Sometimes we have to be a little selfish. We have to protect our feelings and our hearts. Not only that, but...we have to protect ourselves and our bodies as well...and set our emotions apart.

This means that we have to have more respect for ourselves then anyone else. Think about it...if you don't respect yourself, do you honestly think that anyone   else will? Once you have done that, no one will ever be able to make you feel like you are "no good".

Relationships are about give and take...and take and give.

If you keep making sacrifice after sacrifice after sacrifice and you're not getting any in return...then its time to let it go...and this will suffice.

Love overcomes all obstacles and when someone realizes that they really love you, and that they love you for who you are (to include all your baggage...lets face it ladies...we know we are hard to deal with at times) then they too, will make the same sacrifices for you.

They will begin to show you their love, instead of preach about their love.

My grandmother always told me not to take any wooden nickels...

Russian Roulette

They say that the eyes are the door to the soul.
And so…
Here I stand,
Looking at this young woman before me.
Trying to understand,
What it is that I see.

Deep inside…
I'm looking deep inside her eyes.
Trying to figure her out,
Trying to see what it is that makes her weak.
What is it that makes her speak?
What is she all about?

Who is she, where did she come from?
And why does she resemble the mere appearance of me?
Is she soft spoken with a vital token on how to live life and be free?
Or is she just some loud mouth girl who finds pleasure in conquering life's
disputes and claiming them as her forbidden treasure?

What is her purpose…
…her destiny?
Could I be letting her get the best of me?
When she takes one step,
I take two steps moving forward.
And every time I feel like I'm getting ahead,
She's right behind me making me move even more.

See…life is like a game of Russian roulette.
You either hit or miss.
And every time I hear that click and grasp the fact that "life" has just pulled the
trigger and missed.
I take that opportunity as a gift,
And continue on my journey to success…
…to being blessed…
To define who I am and to making a change.
Hoping my positive influence will get trapped in some young kid's brain.
Leaving them to pick up where I left off.

Hoping they will remain tough and never get soft,
Cause this game of Russian roulette stays on and…never gets switched off.

Take heed…
Cause while I'm trying to proceed,
I still feel the need…
To understand,
This woman in front of me, from where she stands.

Who is she, where did she come from?
I'm trying to figure her out.
What makes her weak?
What makes her speak?
What is she all about?

No sooner than I ask myself these questions…
I take a deeper much longer look at this woman standing in front of me.
And I realize,
She is just an utter reflection of me.

But guess what?
I'm caught up.
Life has just pulled the trigger
And this time, instead of it being a miss…
It's a hit.
Now it's your turn to follow through and continue,
On this mission of mentorship and positive influence.
To further shape and mold the youth into a broader, brighter, superior being.
Know what I mean…

Secrecy

Sworn to secrecy.
No one to tell...
An unwalked path, and misled trail.
Silence unbroken,
Words unspoken.
Sworn to secrecy with no explanation.

Survival Skills

I am inspired by the wise
My faith lies only in God and my abilities
My motivation is always set high
And my determination is what allows me to survive.

That Woman

"SHE" was created from "HE"
It was "SHE" who was put here to cherish the man, love the man, stand by the man, and walk with the man.
It was "HE" who is supposed to protect, provide, love, and be strong for "the woman."

As a woman…am I asking for too much?
Asking too much from "the man"…
…the fathers of our children,
Brothers of our sisters, sons of our mothers, and leaders of our society.

I am that woman who challenges that man.

I, as a woman, refuse to be a statistic of another woman whom you, "the man", categorize as being fragile, brittle, and usable.
I am that woman who thrives off of ambition and survives off of love and life itself. Never to fall into that percentage of women who allow themselves to be disrespected, misunderstood, taken advantage of, and discouraged…never encouraged.

My motive is to remain gentle, delicate, and submissive to the opposite gender.
However, I will not become that woman who falls into lust's trap, life's complications, and the man's overbearing ego.

You can be misleading!
For all the wrong reasons…
You mislead me…us. Speaking of what you want, how you want it, and from whom you are going to get it.
And when I resist, disagree, or no longer want to commit to your wish…
…you are so quick to yell out "Slut, whore, and…"
Go ahead…scratch that itch…
Because you are the one who created that image.

I am that woman who walks with strides of confidence.
Every step balanced positively by faith and motivation.
Never will I trip from the negative energy that surrounds me.
But, in case I do…I will pick myself up gracefully,
And continue on my journey of bliss, determination, and happiness.

I will do whatever it takes to remain a success.
Keeping things intact with who I am spiritually, religiously, and individually.
Only to maintain the vision of knowing that someday,
Some young girl will grow to be just like me
Striving to make a difference and keeping up the legacy of being "that woman."

Mental Orgasm (Intellectual Conversation)

Identify my language…
Taste me with your individuality…
Enlighten me…
Instruct me on how to be familiar with your likes and your dislikes
Gently tickle me with your point of views
Caress my thoughts
Trace my opinions with your intellectual erection of hopeful beliefs
Stimulate my thought process by licking my curiosity

Or how about you undress me…
Slowly taking off every layer of my outer appearance so that it's easier for you to get inside me

Spit verse after verse after verse of your prolific "game"
Unbutton my wonders and unzip my questions
Commence to foreplay so that I can finally reach my breaking point
I'm getting higher and higher and the feeling is super intense

Please believe me when I say that it takes a "not so average" man
To teach me the rhythm of his forbidden deep stroke of…lustful thrusts
of…trustful such…penetrating, mind-blowing, sensual conversation

Knowledge is oh so very arousing…
Let's discuss history, anthropology, and philosophy
Let's converse on art, politics, world crisis, dreams and such

Please me…
Continue to tease me…with every…single…verb, adjective, and noun
As you put them together and make complete sentences
Which you add to hours of astonishing discussions

Let's exchange numbers
Cause I can't stand to allow this to exist as a one night stand
I wanna turn my friend into my man
Cause only a real man knows how to excite my sweet spot

Make my knees shake and quiver
Only a real man knows how to deliver this type of satisfaction

Let's chat about any and everything
As long as you keep yourself deep within my brain
We can talk about whatever you wanna talk about
As long as you keep it interesting
As long as you can keep my attention
As long as you speak words of such wisdom and allow me to kiss
every…single…letter of every…single…word that escapes your bittersweet
tongue…
Make my syrupy juices rush to the one part of my body that…
…builds my inner character…
…that sophisticates my whole being

I promise you that I will take you there too
And lead you on a trail to that ultimate high that only we…us…you and I
…can only get from this stimulating…profound conversation

What happened?

What happened to all the men???? I'm talking about a real man! A purpose driven, soul searching, goal achieving, honest, loyal, God fearing, bible quoting man. A man who is not afraid to go after what he wants in life. A man who will do whatever it takes to be successful. A man who isn't afraid to commit to a woman who is on the same level as he. Whatever happened to the men who weren't afraid to make their relationships work. The men who gave a lot, knowing that they would get a lot in return. Whatever happened to the men who were never afraid to show their lady romance and true love? The men who could look you in the eyes, and express their deepest feelings to you. What happened to the men who always knew how to be a gentleman, and never disrespected a woman. I cant count how many times I have been called a b**ch or whore, just because I was too independent or didn't want to respond to a man, when he called me "shorty" or "ma" or decided he wanted to grab on something that didn't belong to him. Excuse me...but I have a name. I was raised by a woman, who taught me how to be just that...A WOMAN! I know how to be a lady and expect to be treated like a woman. We women don't get turned on by your fake pick up lines. Every once in awhile we like to hear "excuse me miss. What's you name? My name is...and you caught my attention by..." We don't want to hear about how big our butts are, or what you want to do to us...those things do not phase us...or at least not us real women. Instead of living your life by what these fake rappers are talking about or how you THINK they live their life...how about you get up and make some changes to yourself. Maybe you will be blessed enough to get a woman like me. Be something...do something, because I refuse to give birth to a child and allow him to grow up like you. I know a woman can never raise a boy to be a man, but I will sure enough die trying cause…I…am definitely disgusted by what I see in our everyday society....and that goes for those sad, WANNA BE women too.

A Letter Written From a Woman…To A Man

To love me, is to love all of me.
Love me from the roots of my hair,
Down to the arch of my feet.

Love my beauty from within…
The beauty from within that exudes through my skin,
And presents the image of who I really am and…
Love me because I am your best friend.
Love the way that I maintain myself, hip to all the latest looks, styles, and trends.
Just to keep your fondness, inquisitiveness, and attention.

Love me because I am a twist between being that extraordinary-go getta-one in a
million-stimulating your mind cause I'm so fine-but at the same time…
I keep you interested with my intellectual words that reveal my intellectual
thoughts, which leads to inconceivable talks…and I leave you wondering.

Love me because I am me…
Love me because I am your backbone,
Your rock & your muse.
When you hurt,
I hurt.
When you cry,
I cry harder.

Love me because God has blessed me with so much strength,
That I am able to overcome an enormous amount of pain,
Pain inflicted upon me by so many of this world's adversities, that it's literally
driving me insane.

Love me because I am the potential mother of your child…
Having to endure nine month of discomfort, numerous hours of labor, and a
lifetime of gratification.
Gratification because I have achieved the greatest accomplishment of bringing
into this world another me…I shall call her Miracle.

Love my vigorous attitude.
Even if it puts you in a "this woman is getting on my nerves" type of mood.
Love my eccentricity, my charisma, and my loyalty.

Love me because I have faith in you.
Love the fact that I am your #1 supporter.
And most importantly,
Love the fact that I was put here to complete you…

Unconditional Love

You don't have to say the exact words
"I Love You", in order for me to believe it.
Cause when it comes down to it....
It's your warm embrace that I feel and
your words of encouragement that I hear.
It's the way you kiss my forehead,
and the way you show nothing but concern.
It's the way you're always there for me no matter what.
It's your actions instead of your words that I believe.
Because of these, I know you love me unconditionally.

My Own Skin

Sometimes I feel too comfortable in my own skin
I need a change…
My character has become too plain
Average…
The same as the day when I first discovered it was time for me to put one foot in front of the other,
Walking in the direction towards a correction

To my recollection,
My demeanor and my speech
Is far less prestigious than the successor that I had planned to be
My thought process is not as deep

Does that mean that I have become a victim in my own skin?
Hiding behind the "yesterdays" and "what I could have been"

No!
I refuse to remain the same
And be named as a victim in my own skin
I demand change

I aspire to become a legacy… an idol
I need to push through so that I can be that prototype of a role model
I need to redefine and reconstruct my own skin
So that I can be proud of whom I have become, from within
And improve on my existence as a woman

Meeting You

Deep in my deliberation…asking myself a survey of questions
And within this survey was a reflection of the who's who and
Which one of those who's I would like to meet

Normally I would think of the most inspiring influential individuals,
But upon my thoughts I felt that if I didn't become acquainted with these three
Then my journey will begin on the brink of defeat

So with that being said…
I would rather not meet one single individual
Instead,
I'd rather meet the things that most people would consider to be impossible

Endurance
Will power
Passion

If I could attain these qualities right now,
At my young age I'd be a powerful entity
Strengthening my identity

I dream of seizing them!
Knowing that I already possess the intelligence and tact to seek them
Makes it a bit intolerable
And knowing that I should already possess these qualities
Makes it hard to swallow
And fathom

All I know is that I would rather be living with them
Teaching others to strive for them
But for now I can only speak of them
And I guess all I can say is…
I long for the day when I will actually meet them

Love Sick

From the minutes to the hours,
From the hours to the days,
And from the days to the weeks.
I'm thinking of you and the things we used to do.

I'm starting to feel my stomach contract with pain,
And the acidulous fluid begins to rise,
And rise,
And rise again.
I want so much to escape from this jail cell of defeated love.
I want so many of my feeling to be sent far away attached to the wings of an
innocent white dove.

But my heart, my soul, and my mind refuse to let go.
My conscience is telling me…"be strong baby girl…move on!"
And my God is blessing me…"My child, I bestow courage and strength upon
you!"

But what is a woman like me supposed to do?
I'm caught up in this wicked game called **LOVE**.

I'm still sleeping on the same side of the bed that you used to.
I no longer feel secure and comfortable.
Instead I'm wrapped up in layers upon layers of sheets and comforters.
And when I dream…
I dream they are you.

All I can do is reminisce,
About your kiss,
Your smile,
Your touch,
Your lips,

I remember the first time we held hands.
The first time we danced,
And the first time we experienced pure romance…

…together!

You loved me,
Then you left me.
And then you loved me again.
Only to leave me hanging in the mist of our eternal sin.

I dream about the times that we laid in the mysterious silence of the night.
Lying there until the first crack of light shined through the window so bright.
Oh how I used to love the way you wrapped me up in your arms as we slept.

But hey…

Guess what?

I'm not in the business of keeping a man that doesn't wanna be kept.

You do you…
And I'm gonna definitely do me.

Because only I can change the slick,
Heartbroken,
Shuck and Jive effects of being love sick.

If these walls could talk

If these walls could talk
They would be able to tell you how many nights I've cried myself to sleep
The countless conversations I've had,
Whether they were good or bad

If these walls could talk
They would be able to tell you how many people have crossed over the threshold
and entered my life
Only to walk right back out with my heart in hand
They would be able to explain the numerous soliloquies
And read to you all the sonnets that I put together in my notebook

If these walls could talk
They would reveal to you my thoughts
They would talk about
How sometimes it seems like enough is never really good enough
Or how pleasing it is for peace to take over and ease my household…my body,
These walls that I use as barriers to protect my body
And my heart
As well as my mine

See, sometimes it's easy for a girl to go insane
And if these walls could talk
My brain would send thousands of signals from the pain through my nerves and
veins
And force these walls to tell you all about it

But for now…I'll let my pen do all of the explainin'
…starting with the pain
Down to my nerves and my veins
then my soliloquy…
All the way down to the sonnets in my notebook

Sweet Sixteen

I am so sick and tired
Of hearing about how I look like a child
I'm 25 going on 26
And everyone keeps talking about how I look like I'm six-teen
I don't think I look young at all
I actually think that I look my age

I think that the younger generation is too busy trying to look my age
Little "Miss" is supposed to be all prissy and innocent
But instead she's too busy trying to act above her age

The average teen girl these days are dress up in outfits that look obscene
Wearing enormous amounts of MAC, Cover girl, and Maybeline
All up in grown folks business
Listening to grown folks conversation

Society has accepted that fact
But I refuse to accept that…
And you wonder why these 36 year old men are getting themselves caught up
With these girls acting, dressing, and talking like they're 26
When they're only six-teen

If you want to play the role of a woman much older,
Be a little bolder and do some of the things that we grown folks do
Pay a bill or two
Work an extremely long eight hours
Come home just in time to cut on the news
And you see the headline of a young girl just- like- you
Who fell victim to an unwanted sexual act
Walking the streets during the late night hours
Dressed all scantily clad, thinking she had the power
To do whatever she liked
Passing by an alley without any street lights
No body heard her scream and shout
Little "Miss Sweet Sixteen" passed out
Waking up in a hospital an few hours too late
Only to find out that she had been raped

The Significance of History (My President)

My president is more than just black and/or white

My president is history
Hope and change
I don't need you to go down the list for me,
Explaining to me how many parts black or white is he

The significance of this history
Is the fact that he made you feel like you could change
From being that simple plain Jane
Or Joe
Running behind every friend or foe
He made you feel like you could do much better

My president is eloquence
So eloquent that he could break things down into the simplest form
So that every non educated and/or educate with honors human being could
understand it

My president is the face of Dr Martin Luther King
He inspired faith and dreams
With the grace of a real king…my president…
…The 44th President of the United States
Made me and you…feel like we can make history too
And so my journey begins…

I may not walk in the path of a civil rights activist
Or become the president of the United States
But among a few of those whom we consider to be great
My president is one of them
And he too, empowered me to go beyond what's been written in my history's
past

Flaws and All

I love the way you kiss me on my neck during one of those gentle embraces
And even though they're just a few simple pecks
I can't help but to get this warm feeling inside
A feeling that makes me feel as if our bodies are communicating to each other
It's like you're telling me that you love me and I'm telling you that I love you
without either of us verbally speaking a word to one another

The order of conversation goes a little something like this…
During the embrace and immediately after you kiss my neck with a few simple
pecks
You release a refreshing breathe that signifies your comfort,
This then commences a cool burst of warm security that rushes up my spine and
causes me to hug you tighter

And I must admit that I love to watch you smoke
Even if it is the one imperfection that I dislike the most
I love that calm, concentrated, deep in thought look you get
While you inhale and exhale
Pause…
And inhale and exhale
On those long sticks of Newport smokes

You get this look that indicates to me that you're brainstorming on something
similar to those "get rich quick" schemes
Only yours is legit…
Because as a future business man
You refer to them as future business plans
And this allows me to recognize
Your entrepreneurial traits and skills that you have internalized
And disguised under…all…of…that…

"My, my, my" is the praise that we women give when we witness…all…of…that

And I love the way you force all of your XXL, 180+ pounds (give or take a few) of
nothing but muscle into my size LARGE, extra comfy men's tee which you stole
from me
I like to think that your only need for it was so that you would have something to
remind you of me whenever I wasn't around

Cause I know that my body leaves just a hint of my sweet smelling pheromones
on each article of clothing that I wear and own
And I know that whenever you're near that tee
It immediately makes you think of me

I love the fact that whenever you lift weights at the gym
You're always wearing a shirt that seems to be two sizes to small
In fact
My favorite one is the Georgia Bulldogs' tee with the sleeves cut off
I don't even care that my girls are teasing and chatting to me about your small
tee
Cause I'm somewhere admiring the view from a distance and at the same time
I'm giving thanks that this 180+ pounds (give or take a few) of nothing but
muscle, skill, and intellect is all mine

But what I love the best
Is that I could be dressed down in baggy sweats, tee, and that infamous purple
head wrap scarf
Cooking you bacon, grits, and scrambles eggs…with cheese of course
On an early Sunday morning right before we get ready for church
And you could care less because you still think that I am beautiful

To be loved and to be in love is such a wonderful feeling

Reconstructed Love

How can you mend a broken heart?
    Many would say that the damage is done
    And "What's done, is done!"
    There's no turning back or looking back

This time we should focus on the process of progression
Instead of taking a step backwards into regression

Why must we be in denial and disallow our relationship and friendship the
opportunity to grow
    Why point the finger to where we don't see change in each other
    When we could be changing each other
    We could be influencing the most influential things
    And encouraging the most courageous beings in each other

We can go far beyond the depths of shattered hearts
    If we learn to manipulate our own pessimistic tactics
    Enabling us to construct a new passion for each other

Let's not limit ourselves to this box of immovable skepticism